NATIONAL GEOGRAPHIC
School Publishing

D0503703

Trabajos

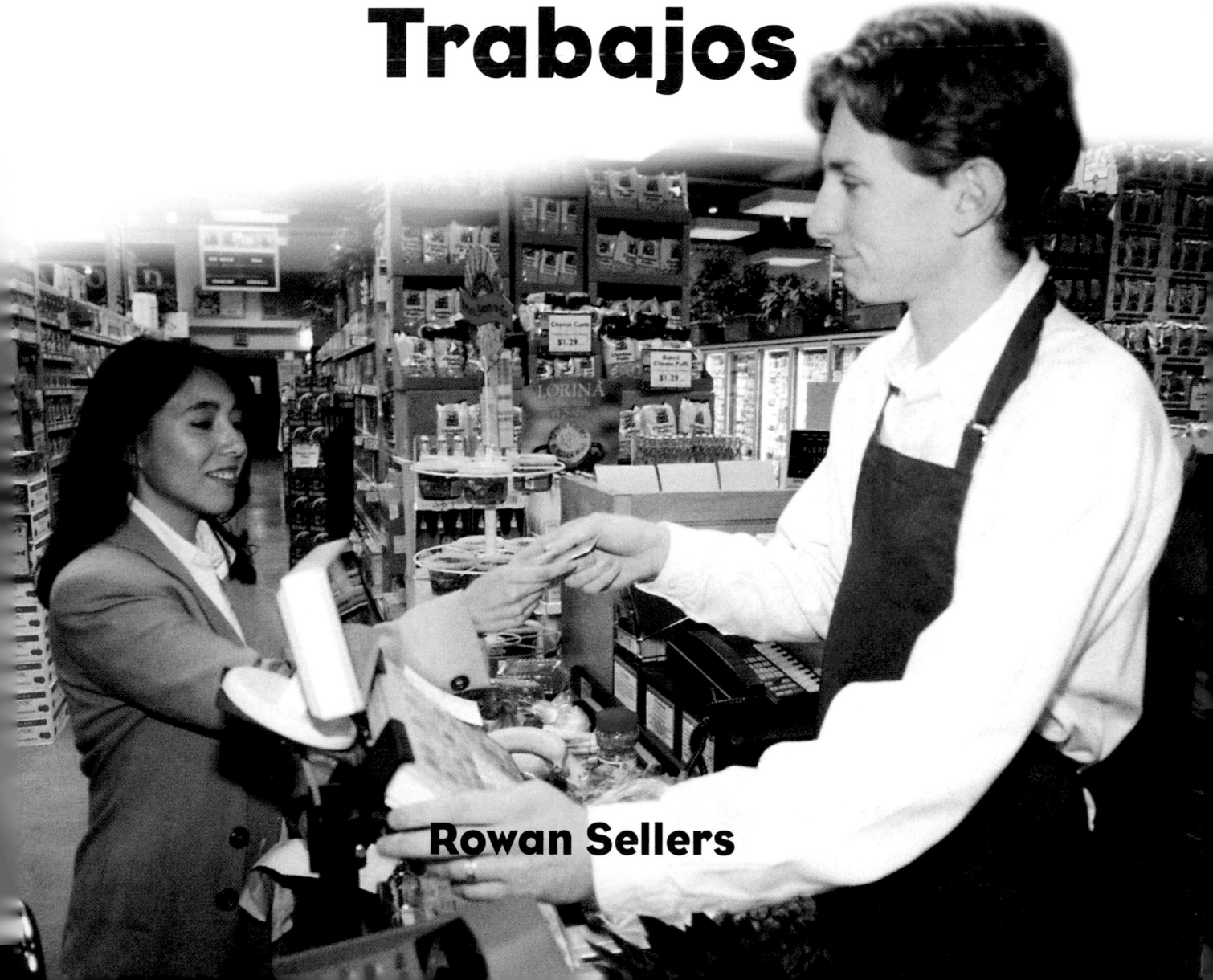

Rowan Sellers

PICTURE CREDITS
Illustrations by David Legge (4–5, 14–15).
Cover, 1, 2, 6 (all), 7 (right), 8 (right), 9 (all), 10 (below right), 12 (all), 13 (all), 16 (all except bottom), Photolibrary.com; 7 (left), 11 (below right), 16 (bottom), APL/Corbis; 8 (left), Jeff Greenberg/PhotoEdit, Inc.; 10 (above left), Getty Images; 11 (above left), APL.

Produced through the worldwide resources of the National Geographic Society, John M. Fahey, Jr., President and Chief Executive Officer; Gilbert M. Grosvenor, Chairman of the Board.

PREPARED BY NATIONAL GEOGRAPHIC SCHOOL PUBLISHING
Ericka Markman, Senior Vice President and President Children's Books and Education Publishing Group; Steve Mico, Senior Vice President and Publisher; Marianne Hiland, Editorial Director; Lynnette Brent, Executive Editor; Michael Murphy and Barbara Wood, Senior Editors; Bea Jackson, Design Director; David Dumo, Art Director; Margaret Sidlowsky, Illustrations Director; Matt Wascavage, Manager of Publishing Services; Sean Philpotts, Production Manager.

SPANISH LANGUAGE VERSION PREPARED BY NATIONAL GEOGRAPHIC SCHOOL PUBLISHING GROUP
Sheron Long, CEO; Sam Gesumaria, President; Fran Downey, Vice President and Publisher; Margaret Sidlosky, Director of Design and Illustrations; Paul Osborn, Senior Editor; Sean Philpotts, Project Manager; Lisa Pergolizzi, Production Manager.

MANUFACTURING AND QUALITY MANAGEMENT
Christopher A. Liedel, Chief Financial Officer; George Bounelis, Vice President; Clifton M. Brown III, Director.

BOOK DEVELOPMENT
Ibis for Kids Australia Pty Limited.

SPANISH LANGUAGE TRANSLATION
Tatiana Acosta/Guillermo Gutiérrez

SPANISH LANGUAGE BOOK DEVELOPMENT
Navta Associates, Inc.

Published by the National Geographic Society
Washington, D.C. 20036-4688

Copyright © 2008 National Geographic Society. All rights reserved. Reproduction of the whole or any part of the contents without written permission from the publisher is prohibited. National Geographic, National Geographic School Publishing, National Geographic Windows on Literacy and the Yellow Border are registered trademarks of the National Geographic Society.

ISBN: 978-0-7362-3837-3

Printed in the U.S.A.

19 18 17 16

10 9 8 7 6 5 4

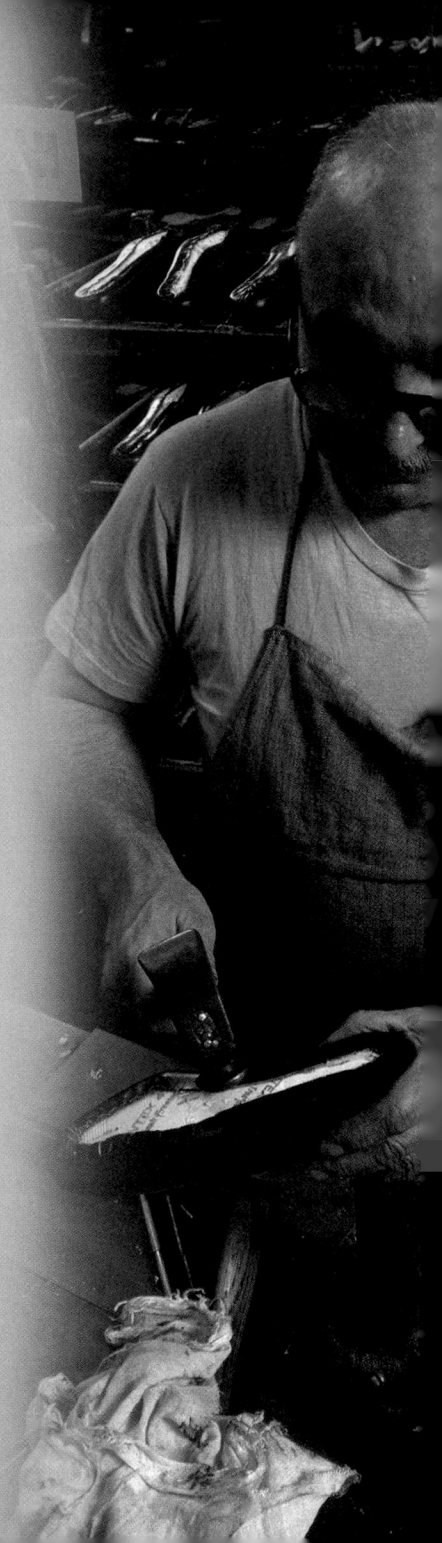

Contenido

Pensar y conversar	4
Salud	6
Seguridad	7
Aprender	8
Hacer	9
Vender	10
Construir	11
Otros trabajos	12
Usar lo que aprendieron	14
Índice ilustrado	16

Pensar y conversar

Busquen a las personas que están trabajando. Hablen sobre el trabajo que están haciendo.

Salud

Algunas personas nos ayudan a estar saludables.

médico

dentista

Seguridad

Algunas personas nos ayudan a estar seguros.

oficial de policía

bombero

Aprender

Algunas personas nos ayudan a aprender.

Hacer

Algunas personas hacen cosas que necesitamos.

Vender

Algunas personas venden cosas que necesitamos.

vendedor de ropa

cajero

Construir

Algunas personas construyen cosas que necesitamos.

albañiles

constructores de puentes

Otros trabajos

Las personas también tienen muchos otros trabajos. ¿Qué otros trabajos se les ocurren?

música
cocineros
agricultor

Usar lo que aprendieron

¿Qué trabajo están realizando estas personas? ¿En qué les gustaría trabajar a ustedes?

ayuda

personas

trabajador

trabajar

trabajo

Índice ilustrado

bombero 7

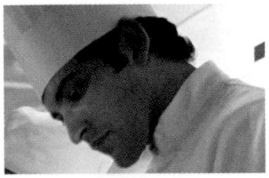

cocinero. 13

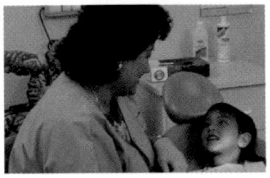

dentista. 6

maestra 8

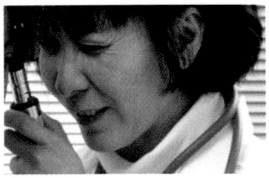

médico 6

oficial de policía. 7